COVID COUPLE

Karen Pleban

authorHOUSE

AuthorHouse™
1663 Liberty Drive
Bloomington, IN 47403
www.authorhouse.com
Phone: 833-262-8899

Published by AuthorHouse 04/29/2024

ISBN: 979-8-8230-2540-9 (sc)
ISBN: 979-8-8230-2538-6 (e)

Library of Congress Control Number: 2024907785

Print information available on the last page.

Any people depicted in stock imagery provided by Getty Images are models, and such images are being used for illustrative purposes only. Certain stock imagery © Getty Images.

This book is printed on acid-free paper.

Because of the dynamic nature of the Internet, any web addresses or links contained in this book may have changed since publication and may no longer be valid. The views expressed in this work are solely those of the author and do not necessarily reflect the views of the publisher, and the publisher hereby disclaims any responsibility for them.

The Beginning

It was Mother's Day, May 12, 1946, when I was born in Cleveland, Ohio. Growing up, my family faced financial struggles, but my oldest sister always looked out for me. My father, a World War II veteran, had a troubled past and battled alcoholism According to my grandmother, my mom received notice that my dad was missing in action during World War II. As it turned out, he was not missing in action, but a prisoner of war detained in a concentration camp. Eventually, he and his troop escaped the camp and was found just after my mother received the "missing in action" notice.

It was not uncommon for my dad to drink anything he could get his hands on, as he was an alcoholic. I once witnessed him drinking radiator fluid when he didn't have any money I witnessed my dad suffering from Delirium Tremens (DTs) several times when I was around seven years old., There is no way to describe how terrible it was. It is difficult to see your father shiver vigorously on the floor with vomit rolling out of his mouth while screaming things like the Nazis are attacking you. There was an incident when we were in our home when he attempted to set it on fire, thinking that we were the enemy. As a result of my father's issues with drinking and the backlash of the war, my parents became separated on and off throughout my life. I never really got to spend much time with him, Nonetheless, my dad would tell me stories about his war experiences when I had the opportunity to sit with him. My mother would get very angry with him when he told me the stories. There were sometimes times when I felt like I was the only one listening to him. It was interesting to hear about some of the things he told me. Despite how long ago he told them, the stories still resonate with me.

During times of sobriety, my father tried to act like a normal husband and father but his illness always interfered. I remember him forcing my sisters to scrub the floors all around the house with a toothbrush while he was in the house. He would have my brother go on the streets to shine shoes for extra money, he told him that he needed the money to help with food, but he would instead use it to buy wine. I was fortunate enough to escape the wrath of most of his episodes.

It was obvious to me that he had a purple heart and a

few other medals because he told me about them. As the years have passed, my dad's military medals were never to be found. I don't recall ever seeing his medals throughout the years. The medals were finally obtained in 2015 after I wrote to the U.S. Department of Defense

One of my brothers was a year younger than me, my oldest brother was three years older, and I had two sisters who were older than me. Throughout my life, my oldest sister always looked out for me. I think she thought of me as a baby doll since we couldn't afford dolls, toys, or bikes for her.

As a result of our poverty, we were raised in the projects. We lived among all kinds of criminals and thieves. As a result of my sister's friendship and my sister's protection, I have always been safe.

I remember my mother always kept the shades down during holidays like Christmas to conceal the fact that we were poor. Having good food at Christmas was a thrilling experience at our house. As kids, we all made each other something for Christmas. I remember one year my sister made me a baby doll out of old socks.

When I was around seven years old, my aunt and uncle took me to Atlantic City with them because my mom had trouble getting me to gain weight. My Aunt and Uncle fed me all kinds of stuff in Atlantic City. I had a great time and I gained weight.

Because we were destitute, attending school was difficult. As a kid, I was teased for having hand-me-down clothes and being ridiculed by kids when they saw my dad drunk.

We were only 9 years old I got into a huge physical fight with one of my neighbors named Katie because she was teasing me about how she saw my drunken father and that we were going to have a poor easter. Katie and I had our first communion together. My sister Rose supervised the fight to keep it fair without other kids jumping in on it. It turned out to be a draw because the fight went on for over an hour and neither one of us would quit. We both got scratched up, our hair pulled out and our clothes ripped up. My sister Rose got into a lot of trouble with my mother over that one. Shortly after that fight, my mother got a job, and we moved out of the projects never to look back again. She didn't have any skills, but she got a job cooking for a local bar. That is when she started drinking a lot.

My younger brother Chuck and I looked like twins until we were 10 years old. Despite being only a year apart in age, we had a lot in common. Both my sisters got married, while my older brother spent a lot of time with his friends. My brother Chuck and I were always hanging out together. Together with him and his friends, I used to fish at Lake Erie. During our school days, we would spend a lot of time in the schoolyard. I missed him terribly when he joined the Navy once he turned sixteen. As a result, my mother and I were the only ones at home. Only at night or on Sunday mornings would I be able to see my mother, nor did I have much adult supervision. As part of my chores, I ironed clothes, washed and dried dishes, and sometimes mopped the floors. Additionally, I earned money babysitting to help out with the household expenses.

I don't recall too much interaction with my mother while I was in grade school. I got most of my attention from my sisters and grandparents.

Later in life just before my teenage years with the help of my grandparents, my mother moved out of the hood and rented a home in a decent area. All five of us children developed a clean life and became productive adults. None of us ever utilized welfare after leaving home.

As a teenager, my life was very different from what it was when I was in elementary school. As a result, I was much more capable of handling myself. It was easy for me to become popular at school and to make many friends. There was always something to do for me. It may have been because we no longer lived in the hood and homes were farther apart.

The 1960s were my teenage years. Music of this caliber was out of this world. I would watch Dick Clark with my two older sisters and dance with them. In the same way that I enjoyed the music from the 60s, I enjoyed the music from the 50s. There was a lot of fun to be had. Driving to drive-in restaurants and watching movies was a common pastime. Friday nights were usually filled with drag racing among the guys. Our regular meeting spot was the drive-in, where we would just hang out. In terms of food, the most popular item was a milkshake and a hamburger or hotdog. As for the French fries, they were always outstanding. My favorite things to do were going to the high school dances and roller skating with my friends. The music was fast-paced, and the musicians were energetic like the Beatles, Mamas and Papas, Elvis, Beach Boys, Ray Charles, Chubby Checkers, and so on. Obesity was not common with the kind of dancing we all did.

During the time my younger brother was in the Navy, I hung out with my older brother's girlfriends until I met my older brother's buddy Ron, whom I later got married to ... Playing chess and cards with my older brother during free time was something I really enjoyed.

Childhood Sweetheart

1960 I was 14 when I met my husband-to-be through my older brother Fred. His name was Ron. This guy had a terrific build and drove a 1956 blue and white Ford Fairlane convertible. Several months later I found out that this Ron guy was a bodybuilder and was featured in Muscle Man magazine in the past.

One day, I was returning home from school with my friend Louise when we noticed Ron and my brother sitting on the porch of my house. She commented on the good-looking guy who was at my house with my brother, but I shrugged it off because after all he was my brother's friend, and I didn't think he would have an interest in me anyway.

We lived in an old colonial home that my mother had rented. In it was a bench-type seat that ran across the window with a closed-in bookshelf on each side. One day after school my brother came home with his buddy Ron to hang out at the house and wash Ron's car. I was sitting at that window watching the squirrels in the tree and suddenly Ron sat next to me and asked me what I was doing. I told him I was watching the cute squirrels. I was very uncomfortable talking to him because he was so good-looking in addition to the fact that I knew he was going steady with some girl that I went to school with. To my surprise, he asked me if I would go on a date with him. I thought my brother put him up to do that to make fun of me. So naturally, I turned him down and went about my business. I was popular in school so there was no boredom in my life. I loved dancing and had lots of friends.

After several months went by, one Friday night I was preparing for a great night out at the school dance with a few of my friends. They were supposed to pick me up that late afternoon to take me to that dance with another girlfriend of mine. When I came out of the bedroom to get ready for the dance, I discovered both my brother and his friend Ron sitting on my front porch. I went to join them while waiting for my friends to show up. They never showed up and I was very angry that they stood me up and I was embarrassed in front of Fred and Ron. Ron took advantage of the moment and asked me to join him and my brother with my brother's girlfriend to hang out with them. He said like a double date thing. I thought, "What the heck else I am going to do? We had a great time. Went to a drive-in movie and the next day we went to the lake and did some fishing. On Sunday, we just hung out around the house listening to music while he was waxing his car in our yard.

That following Monday, I returned to school angry that my two friends stood me up. When I confronted them, they said they did arrive at my home on Friday to pick me up only to be greeted by my brother and his friend (Ron) who told them that I had other plans. Unreal!! They must have shown up while I was getting dressed in the bedroom., I was only upset with my brother and Ron for a few moments because my girlfriends pointed out how cute it was that they circumvented my date to get me hooked up with Ron. From that moment on Ron became an important part of my life.

We spent a lot of time together for the next 4 years. While I was attending high school, he was attending electronics school with his father. He was an only child and had a lot of love from his mother and father. They were like an ideal family. I came from a family with 5 kids. Not much money because my mother had to raise all five of us kids alone without financial support. There was a time when she was on welfare and received food stamps, but it was taken away from her when my grandparents gave her a car and a TV. I had a younger brother and an older brother along with 2 older sisters. My father was a World War II vet with mental problems from the war. Both my parents had drinking problems and they separated by the time I was a teenager. By then both my sisters and older brother got married. I had to get a babysitting job when I was 12 to help put food on the table.

Ron and I didn't go out on fancy dates. My high school socializing came to a stop when I met Ron because we spent most of our time together studying his electronics and watching Friday night movies on TV at his house. I enjoyed studying electronics with him I made a game with the use of the ohms law. Loved reading the resisters. Ron introduced me to weightlifting so we worked out in his makeshift gym in his basement. At that time, I weighed 110 pounds. Our outings consisted of walking and playing with our dogs at the parks, fishing or just driving around. Our dogs became best friends also. Lucky was a female German shepherd that belonged to Ron and Sailor was a male black long hair retriever that belonged to me. Ironically, I was gifted Sailor by an ex-boyfriend. Sailor was very devoted to me. Ron and I enjoyed being with each other. We used to talk about having kids when we got married. Our ideal family would be 2 boys and a girl. The girl would be last so that she would have the two boys protect her when she grew up and be beautiful.

As it turns out, we got married in April 1964. It was a small wedding. We were not about frills and stuff, so I wore a nice blue suit and Ron wore dress pants and shirt and we married at the justice of the piece. Of course, my mother didn't approve of this type of wedding, but she couldn't afford a big one anyway. She wanted me to get married in a White gown with a veil at a Catholic church. There was no way we could have afforded a wedding like this. My mother did hold a reception for us at her house.

As soon as we got married, we opened a TV – Radio repair shop next to his uncle's jewelry store. A week after we were married, we were involved in an automobile accident and were struck by a hit-skip driver without insurance and totaled our only car. Ron was pushed through the windshield and ended up with a concussion. I was thrown against the dash and suffered internal injuries. We managed to get another car and we struggled with the TV shop for about a year.

Our first son was born a year and 1 month after we were married. The business did not provide enough to raise a family so we decided it was financially best to give up the business so Ron could get a job. We continued the business part-time out of his parent's basement and Ron obtained a job with benefits so that we could be that perfect family we so often talked about.

Our firstborn was a boy in 1965. While in the hospital

with the birth of our first son, Ron had the biggest red roses delivered to the hospital. I was the proudest woman in the world. I was proud of my handsome husband, beautiful flowers, and the most perfect-looking baby in the world.

Things were like a roller coaster because my mother became very ill with cancer during my pregnancy with my second son. My brothers, sisters and I took turns taking care of her during her last days. In the meantime, my father came to live with us for a while. We were not aware of the reasons my father would act up. He would act like he was in the war. He would say crazy things scaring my son Ronnie. I finally had to have my sister take my dad because it was difficult handling him while I was pregnant. Many years later after he passed, we learned that he suffered PTSD from World War II. Back then that condition was not known as it is today.

While Ron was at work, my son and I would go sit with my mother to help take care of her because she was suffering from terminal cancer. She loved her grandson very much. She passed away on Halloween night in 1969.

A month and a half after my mother passed away in 1969, we had our second son. Another beautiful baby was born, and our oldest son gave his young brother the name Eddie. So, this baby's name was Edward John. A beautiful dozen roses were delivered to the hospital from

Ron and our family plan was falling into place just like we had talked about when we were dating.

Finally, in 1972, we finished having our children with a beautiful little girl and we named her Barbra Ann. Ron picked the name and since our oldest son provided the name of our youngest son Ed, we used the pronunciation of her name from Ed. He pronounced his sister's name as bar-bra and our older son spelled it. Our entire family was involved in the family name thing. This time Ron had a dozen pink roses delivered to me at the hospital. Our plan for the perfect family was falling into place!! Two brothers follow in Dad's steps and help protect their little sister who is going to follow in Mom's steps.

After coming home from the hospital with our daughter, I noticed a very proud look on Ron's face, and he remarked at the glow I had on my face while holding our newborn daughter and our sons sitting next to me.

We had the perfect family that we wanted. Two boys and a sister. All were beautiful healthy children.

Family Tragedy

As it turns out, our plan for the perfect family was crushed. The boy's sister who was to follow in their mom's steps did not materialize. Our perfect dream broke! When Barbara turned 6 weeks old, we celebrated and took the kids to the drive-in theater. While at the theater Barbra acquired a slight fever. We were not even there for an hour when she started her fever. Ron brought us home right away. I called the emergency room and they said to just give her baby aspirin and she should be ok. But she was not ok. Later that night when I went to check on Barbara, I found her in her crib with fluid rolling out of her nose and mouth and burning an extremely high fever. We rushed her to the emergency room where they recorded her temperature at 108 and they put her in a tub of ice. Her illness went on for 2 years and then We lost our little girl in 1974 from a virus. It was devastating to our family. Words cannot express the pain we all went through. A true strain on our relationship . too much to describe. Her illness started when she was 6 weeks old, resulting in her being critically ill with severe brain damage for the remaining 2 years of her life. It was a constant drain on our emotions She would be released from the hospital and then shortly after return because of breathing issues. She had suffered severe brain damage. Trips to the hospital several times a month, sometimes days apart and sometimes weeks apart. She finally passed in 1974. The phone call informing me of Barbra's passing is one of my most vivid memories. I had expected her to pass by now, so while it was emotionally painful, I was not surprised to hear that she had passed away. When I received the call, Ron was standing next to me, so when I hung up, I looked at him and told him Barbra had passed away. The color of his face became very pale. After losing our daughter, we sobbed with our boys at our side. She was with me twenty-four hours a day while she was at home, and I visited her each day when she was hospitalized, so I think it affected Ron more than anyone else. Since he had to work, he didn't have a chance to give her as much care and love on her as much as I did. Unlike me, he didn't get to hold her as much as I did.

During this trying time, our boys were being neglected and not receiving our proper attention. My husband suffered a sense of being helpless because he felt it was his job, his mission, and his duty to be our protector. I felt somehow, I failed as a mother to not stop this illness. We worked extremely hard to remain solid as a family, but the loss of our daughter was a tragedy that caused a very important missing link in our plans. Throughout the years, we worked hard at trying to keep it together Ron and I would feel the pain in each other's hearts and… we still tried to support each other. However, Ron had succumbed to alcohol and drugs to deal with all the emotions in the family.

After our daughter passed away, Ron noticed me going into a depression of emptiness inside and even encouraged me to go to cosmetology school with my sister. I did go to cosmetology school and almost completed the course, but that did not work out because every little girl's hair I worked on reminded me of how it would have been with my daughter. I ended up dropping out of beauty school. Ron talked me into going to computer school. Back in those days, computers were a man's career. I graduated and continued with a career in the computer field and did well.

As Ron's drinking and drug abuse increased, violent outbreaks began to occur. As a result of his arthritis pain and depression, his doctor prescribed him Percodan and Valium, which made his drinking more problematic. After a while of mixing these prescriptions with alcohol, it caused a split personality with Ron. When Ron mixed these prescriptions with alcohol for a while, he developed a split personality. My boys and I were subjected to a great deal of physical and mental violence from him. My boys were terrified of their dad, and I worried for our lives around him. There was a man inside Ron's body that I was not familiar with. I became genuinely concerned because he had violent mood changes. I was certain it was because of drinking and prescriptions. When I told the doctor about my concerns, the doctor denied that the combination of medication and alcohol affected his mood swings.

As a result of some violent episodes, I would leave him in desperation, only to have him beg me for another chance swearing he would change for the better. Being the father of my boys and loving him so much, I would believe him and come back.

There have been incidents of him shooting a gun in my direction and another time he busted out the driver's side window on my car to stop me from leaving. Another time, he erupted into a violent rage while driving. I slipped on the icy road when he got to a stop sign, trying to get away from him. The car tire was headed straight for my head when I rolled out of the way, but it caught my hand and wrist. The car behind us picked me up and took me to the emergency room. Ron showed up at the hospital shortly after they wrapped my badly bruised arm. As soon as he began scolding me for jumping out of the car, the doctor on duty told him to leave me alone and that he would call the police. With that being said Ron calmed down and took me home.

Our relationship was very unstable, to say the least. This went on until finally, my doctor told Ron that he was killing me from the inside out because of the worries and stress he caused me. Ron cooperated with my doctor and got off those mood-altering medications. Although he finally got off the mood-altering drugs, our relationship was tarnished and weakened. My security of feeling safe with him had decreased considerably and his paranoia increased with age, but our commitment somehow stayed together for the boy's sake. We just had to try and work things out for the sake of our boys!!

We moved out to the county with our two boys. Ron noticed I was very overprotective with the boys. I would not let them do normal boy stuff for fear of them hitting their heads and ending up with brain damage like their sister. He knew he had to do something and circumvented me by getting the boys active with boy stuff. He had them driving tractors at ages 8 and 9... working on cars at ages 10, riding motorcycles at ages 10 and 11. He even had them driving the car in the area at age 10. One of the fondest memories our boys have of their father was when one day, I used Ron's car to go to work. When I left for work, Ron gathered the boys and showed them how to use a torch on my Ford Pinto. the three of them made a dune buggy of sorts out of my car!!! They removed all the windows, doors, tailgate, and hood. They were having fun driving this vehicle all over the terrain jumping the ditches and hills. I was in shock but calmed down when I saw the enjoyment their father and the boys created. I was thrilled to see that they all shared some quality father-son time. My boys still talk about that to this day. Ron was extremely strict with the boys and sometimes seemed mean. Ron was constantly interfering with my wanting to protect the boys from hurting themselves. My oldest son won first place in electrification in the state of Ohio through FFA 3 years in a roll and my youngest son won trophies with woodworking and building in 4 H. They each had a young calf to raise for their project. I'm thankful Ron intercepted my protectiveness to our boys. He was extremely strict with them and at times I thought too strict. But today, those boys are survivors. They can do almost anything they make their mind up to. Both are in the construction field. We compiled a cookbook of my recipes as a family. Having an old TRS 80 computer and binding the books by hand, Ron and the boys helped me compile this cookbook.

When our oldest son turned 18 in 1983, he went into

the Air Force without even telling us, We were devastated. We had no idea where he was. We felt we lost another child. My heart ached and I know Ron had to feel bad, but he stood strong and acted angrier than hurt that his son simply vanished from our lives.

After time passed without our older son, we realized that our oldest son left because we smothered him with too much love. Overprotected him from getting hurt, getting into drugs, and getting in with the wrong friends. It all worked except it made him run away from us.

Realizing our costly mistake with our oldest son causing him to run away, we changed our ways and let the string loose on our youngest son. Perhaps to loose. He ended up in trouble, got into drugs, and hooked up with a bad crowd.

Even though we made horrible mistakes raising our boys. to this day they both realize that we love them very much and I am so very proud of both of them.

A New Direction

As years went on Ron became mellow. We became good friends. Our boys did stay somewhat in touch at a distance of course but Ron and I continued to stick it out together. Ever since our daughter passed, we were no longer lovers. It was like we were in an arrangement of some sort.

When the boys were raised and out of the house, we started to enjoy life differently. Go out to dinner, go dancing. buy the finer things in life. What else did we have? The perfect family we envisioned was broken, and things didn't turn out the way we hoped. As Ron continued to drink, I learned to live with the consequences of his behavior. Ron was working as a journeyman electrician working for a manufacturing company while I was a Computer Specialist for our city.

His job was repairing laser counters for the newspaper industry. He was known in the industry as Laserman.

In 1995 Ron lost his job from a plant shutdown. The company left their customers in the air without support for their laser counters. As a 52-year-old, Ron felt that no one would hire him at that age and began feeling depressed. In an attempt to encourage him, I suggested he start a new company that repairs laser counters, making use of his reputation as Laserman and technical skills. To introduce Ron to the public, he obtained a list of customers from his former employer. We mailed introductory letters to all newspapers in each state. We received a good response from this mail. Because of the good response, we opened our own business at home repairing laser counters for the newspaper industry. I continued to work out of the home while he was doing his business. Of course, I was a big part of the business because I was able to maintain the administrative part of his business. It started to be lucrative, but his drinking interfered with his personality, attitude, and work ethic. The business was lucrative enough to provide us with a nice down payment on a bigger home.

In the year 2000, we moved to a beautiful brick ranch. But Ron no longer conducted his business which reduced our household income. He lost interest. He had to get a job to help with the mortgage, so he got hired as a journeyman electrician at a factory. I continued with my career and moved on to being a Computer Systems Manager for our county.

Ron had a major heart attack in 2002. I was devastated. I thought I lost the love of my life. His five-bypass surgery was followed by a pacemaker implant. The doctor immediately medicated me to calm me down while I was in the emergency room with my husband. All I kept thinking was how hard it was for us all these years. I wished things would have gone as planned when we first got married. My heart was in that hospital bed with him. As he recovered, I was hoping that the original Ron would surface, and we could be deeply in love again. As time passed, the original Ron never did surface and became worse in a different way. He became worthless. No interest except for beer and cigarettes. He was no longer violent, but just like a man in a shell.

Our oldest son visited the hospital the entire time and never let him spend the night alone. My son made sure I went home to get some rest. The youngest son came from Florida to visit his dad.

During one of Ron's follow-up visits with the doctor, I expressed concern about Ron's split personality and how difficult it was to reason with Ron. Ron was very argumentative. The doctor explained that Ron had some dementia going on perhaps due to a lack of oxygen to his brain during his heart attack.

It was challenging taking care of Ron when he came home from the hospital. He refused to stop drinking and smoking. He quit drinking beer and selected wine as his choice of alcohol. He believed that the wine was healthier drinking a 3 Liter box a day instead of a case of beer. Tobacco use was over a pack a day. I also continued to smoke up to a pack a day. In 2008, I quit cold turkey after suffering from upper respiratory infection every year for 5 years.

Life Changing Event

In 2005 I became ill and was diagnosed with LUPUS. I was forced into an early retirement. Due to the sudden loss of income, we had a financial crash, and we lost our two cars. We had to work on correcting our credit and we did. I did pick up a little sidekick job as a quality control field representative, which helped with the groceries.

After we recouped from our financial crash and Ron recouped from his heart attack, we decided to try to enjoy life. We set out to purchase a brand new 24 ft cabin cruiser boat, Cruise Lake Erie, and do some fishing enjoying life to the fullest. We signed up with a campground that had boat ramps and purchased a trailer sitting on a lot. We camped all summer long for several years. When I say camp, I mean we had 2 bedrooms, a nice kitchen and living room and of course a bath. The campground would have events like Bingo, fish fries, steak dinners or what have you. I participated in all of it, but Ron just wanted to stay in the camper and drink his beer and smoke cigarettes. After going out on the boat a few times, Ron said he could no longer enjoy Lake Erie. He just could not take the boat, but he insisted I make the best of it. Ron claimed that the motor of the boat was affecting his pacemaker. So, it was up to me to make use of this boat because it was a brand-new boat that we were making payments on and I was hoping that he would re-gain an interest in it. Ron was proud of how I handled the boat and often bragged about me being the captain. He never regained his desire to go on the boat. However, I did enjoy the boat and took it out on the lake every chance I could.

In 2008, Ron had to rush me to the hospital for an upper respiratory infection. This was an every-year occasion. Every year I would have to go to the emergency room, receive breathing treatment, and upon release from the hospital, light up a cigarette as soon as I got in the car. But this time... I lit my cigarette and looked at that piece of paper with tobacco wrapped around it having control over me. I put the cigarette out and I told Ron enough is enough and I am going to quit smoking. I told him that smoking was controlling my life with my health and financial burden. I put the money I would buy for cigarettes aside and bought a huge 82-inch TV and made the payments with the money I saved from quitting smoking. It was difficult to quit, especially with Ron continuing to smoke in the house. I was determined and I beat the craving, the addiction, and control and remained smoke-free.

The political rift raft on television became Ron's obsession in 2009. The TV talk shows would result in him becoming verbally violent, yelling at the screen and once even pulling out a 9-millimeter gun to shoot it. Fortunately, I was able to intercept it. My patience was wearing thin, and I walked out because it was getting too much for me.

Upon hearing what happened, one of our friends tried to call Ron on the phone, but he would not answer. He was fearful that Ron may be sitting in the house with a heart attack, so he suggested I have the sheriffs do a welfare check. That is what I did, and I regret it. It turned out that Ron had a 12-hour standoff with the sheriffs. Since they recognized that he was difficult to reason with, the sheriffs refused to let me into the house. They knew he had guns in the house because he had a concealed weapon permit, and they feared for my safety. It was horrifying to watch a swat team encircle my house for over 12 hours. Ron was incarcerated because of this. It took six weeks for them to release him. In the end, he was placed on probation for a year after being released. He continued to smoke and drink. But the drinking was very discreet. He was not allowed to be seen that he was drinking.

I authored several books in 2010 to keep myself busy. The first was about our daughter, the second was our family's cookbook rewritten, and the third was about the evolution of computing since cave dweller times.

In 2014 we still owed 5 yrs. on the boat so we decided that since this boat would soon be requiring repairs, we decided to sell it to get out from under the monthly payments and bought a used boat.

I bought a twenty-foot outboard and took all kinds of pictures of me and my friends fishing on the boat, but he did not like the idea of me fighting four-foot waves on Lake Erie with that small boat. He became obsessed with me getting this bigger boat.

In the meantime, my husband has been ailing with a bad heart and a bit of dementia during the last several years of his life. In December of 2014 when I returned home from shopping, my husband greeted me at the door and said "You're an owner of a 24' cabin cruiser boat" He said he bought it with his credit card. I was shocked and didn't know what to do. He would have never done anything like this before he got ill. I wondered if I should call the salesperson and explain to him that my husband has impaired thinking and the deal needed canceling. I just could not do it. It would have broken his heart if

I canceled the deal. Ron was already feeling helpless. I tried to tell him that he should not have bought this boat without looking at it. But he was intent on me having this boat. He even said that he would let me take him to the islands, So I decided to make the best of the situation.

It was a hobby-like project we worked on together. Even though he did not want to go on the boat, he loved talking to me about the boat. We would have daily discussions on what was needed for the boat. We talked about how to manage the boat, going to the islands, etc. We worked together on making new cushions for it. His last project for the boat was fixing a motioning Owl to sit at the dock to keep the big birds from releasing themselves by my boat. I wanted him to have some enjoyment while I would be spending time out on the boat. I got him an English Springer Spanel dog to keep him company while I was out fishing. She was six years old and her name was Lady. I enrolled her into a good citizen school. She turned out to be a very loyal dog. Then we invested in making a radio room for him. He renewed his FCC HAM radio license, we put up antennas and purchased all kinds of radio equipment. But he lost interest in that also.

I had a horrible time getting used to managing this big boat. Every time I took it out, I would return home telling him how disappointed I was that I could not handle it and he would respond with confidence in me that I would eventually handle it. Sure enough, just as he predicted, I finally grasped hold of how to drive this monster and he responded by saying that he knew I could do it.

. Although my husband inspired me to fish, he just could not take the motion on the boat in Lake Erie and was unable to join me but wanted me to continue fishing because he loved perch and walleye. Every time I went out fishing on the boat, I would take pictures of the water, fish, and boat to show him when I got home. I acquired a nice array of friends who would join me on my boat. I had several friends who would go fishing with me on my boat. Celesta my fishing friend met me while I was having a garage sale at my house. She wanted to know if I had fishing rods and if I had already sold them. During our conversation, she said she was disappointed because she used to go fishing with her husband's friends and then one day they told her their wives did not want them to take her out to fish anymore. So, I invited her to go fishing with me. We ended up becoming great friends and she even learned how to be my anchor person.

His appetite has dropped dramatically, and he claimed he was doing it willingly. His temperament was short and always continued to yell at the News on TV. He had a very bad outlook on world affairs, however, anyone you talk to these days had issues with the way things were going in the world with the terrorist attacks. It seemed that we would argue every night. One night I told him that as mean as he is, if he would pass away, I wouldn't feel as helpless as I did when he had his first heart attack. He just laughed at me when I said it.

Alone without Hope

In 2015 My oldest son came to visit us on a surprise visit. We were so pleased to see him! On his last evening at our house, we were all sitting in the living room just conversing and listening to my husband's hot stereo. Our living room had two full couches across from each other with a coffee table in front of them and an 86" TV was at the end of the room. I was on the couch across the room on my laptop playing games while my son and husband were sitting on the couch conversing with one another. Suddenly, my husband broke down in tears and said, Son, I just want you to know how proud I am of you. And my son said, "I know Dad, and I am also proud of you. I held the tears back as I knew in my heart that was a sign of something to come and I noticed my son was getting choked up also. Well, it came time for my son to go home because he had to return to work. As always it was difficult to see him leave but after my son left. I noticed tears in my husband's eyes.

On the 27th of June, Ron (my husband) asked me to make sure I got a pizza delivered to our son Ron for his birthday which was on the 28th. He knew pizza was our son's favorite. So, I arranged to have the pizza delivered just as he returned home from work. Our son called us that evening and thanked us for the pizza and was very excited. Ron told him to enjoy it but advised him to watch his diet and exercise.

The next morning, Ron seemed ill. He said he had cramps and I asked him if he would like to see the doctor or go to the hospital, and he said no, But he fell and I helped him get on the couch. I sat on the other couch across from him. Ron gave a few strokes of petting on his dog Lady. While sitting on the couch with my laptop watching Ron on the other couch across from me, I was typing an email to my oldest son.

Following is the letter I was sent to my son moments before my husband's heart attack

Hi Son,

How was work? Hope it was easy for you!!
Dad fell again today. He has been cramping a lot. I asked him if he had diarrhea, but he said no. Just cramping.

Anyway, he was on his way back from the bathroom and I watched him making his way to the couch. He was wobbly and fell on the floor. I had him lay there for a few minutes while I took advantage of the stuff falling off his coffee table and dusted it. It is hard to dust the table with all his junk because he gets mad at me when I move stuff, so when he fell, he knocked a lot of it off the table and I took advantage of it and cleaned it off.

Anyway, when I was done cleaning it off, I helped him up. It was difficult because he was having a hard time helping me lift him.

I told him to drink some of that Powerade because it has electrolytes in it. He is lying on the couch with an occasional moan. I don't know why he does that. anyway, the reason I told him about the Powerade is that he seems so fragile when he walks and when I was helping him get back on the couch, his arms and legs seemed so cold, so I told him that the Powerade would hydrate him and the electrolytes should make him stronger.

Today I had to go to get my oil changed and hated to leave him alone while he was feeling ill, so when I got to the shop, I told them my husband was ill, and I would appreciate it if they took care of me right away and they did!! I was only gone for an hour.

Well, I just wanted to update you on Dad. I'm so glad you came and spent some time with him. Some day you will be happy you did also.

I love you

Love Mom

No sooner had I finished typing the email and hit the send button, Ron slid off the couch and onto the floor. I ran to help him but Ron's dog Lady, positioned herself by him and tried to stop me from helping him because she thought she was protecting him me. She sensed something was very wrong. I called out his name to get his attention. Lady growled and snarled showing me all her teeth. I had to wrap the leash around her muzzle to stop her from biting me so I can try to help Ron. I did not get a response from Ron, So While hanging on to Lady's muzzle, I dialed 911. I then dragged Lady to the bedroom and locked her in there so that she would not attack the paramedics. By the time I finished locking Lady up, the paramedics arrived and started working on Ron but could not get him to respond. They took Ron to the hospital, and I followed the ambulance. Ron passed away at the hospital with me at his side.

Now my world is very silent. No matter who is around me… It is quiet. Even with voices in the background, music playing, dogs barking… and great friends around me… it still seems silent with background sounds in the distance. Although it doesn't make any sense, the silence in the night is noisy. I started to write a book about Ron during the nights I couldn't sleep.

Occasionally it seemed like I got a sign that he was talking to me. For example: I was thinking about him while driving one day and wondering if he could see me or feel my sadness, the radio volume on my car turned up very loud just like the one in the house would do when he wanted to listen to his stereo, he would crank it up loud. Another example was when I was in the bedroom and noticed his picture on my dresser and I picked it up and said while crying "Ron my heart aches so bad for you and I miss you so much. I don't know what I am going to do or what to do" Just then my dog notified me that she wanted to go out. so I let her out the patio door in the backyard and just as I let her out, one of the little finches that he used to watch feed outside our front bay window flew into the doorway right over my shoulder and landed on the window sill. I put my hand down for the bird to hop on my palm and it did!! I walked across the room with this bird on my palm to the door and gently stuck my hand out the door and told the finch that it could not stay in the house and the finch flew away.

It seems that I have cried every single day for the first month after he passed. My ribs were sore from all the sobbing and my heart felt heavy. So many thoughts ran through my mind. I couldn't even bring myself to board our boat. I'd drive down to the dock and see the owl that he worked very diligently on, and my heart would just ache and I would just leave the marina and return home without boarding the boat. On the first month anniversary of his death. I'm more composed with a lot less crying, but I am still having issues sleeping at night feeling very weak in the knees and feeling very tired. I could easily fall asleep during the day, but I don't want to sleep during the day because I need to sleep at night.

Dreams

One day while I was at the marina, I was approached to volunteer my time and boat for an event at the marina hosting Little Brothers and Little Sisters with a boat ride out on Lake Erie and I gladly accepted the challenge. One of my friends Wendy volunteered to help me with this event and she spent the night at my house because we were to leave early in the morning for the marina. That was the first night that I slept since Ron passed away. But I realized the only reason I slept so well was because I had someone else at the house sleeping in another room. The next night I was home alone again. I had two horrific nightmares that night. The first nightmare I dreamt of was when I woke up from sleeping to find smoke coming out of the floor by my feet with an occasional spark floating. So, I tried to call 911 but the phones wouldn't work. When I ran outside to go to the neighbors, I saw three men just outside my house… and I yelled at them telling them that my house was on fire. I tried to run to one neighbor, but they would not open their door, so I ran to the other neighbor he came to the door, and I told him my house was on fire and he simply walked away from the door and while I was waiting for the fire department and the guys that were hanging around my house dragged me to their car… and I was yelling at them about my house and all they did was look at me and smile and I jumped out of their car and ran to the house and found the firemen there and they had put out the fire and then people were stealing things out of my house! And I woke up…

Then I went back to sleep and dreamt that I was in the car with my husband. I was telling him how much I missed him!!! He just grinned and then I asked why he was here and that he was dead and all he did was grin. I leaned over and kissed him and told him how much I loved him, but he fell forward and was dead again and I stopped the car and pulled him out. He stood up and I yelled at him and asked him why he was doing this and that he was dead… there were people all around us and I kept telling people he was dead… and all he did was look at me with a smile. I was getting angry because he was dead and not acting right and I pushed him and woke up.

Another night I woke up again in tears and recalled the sad dream I had. In this dream, I went and acquired a part-time job to keep me busy working on computerized equipment. But on the first day, I just could not concentrate and discovered myself in a very strange place. No one knew who I was or what I was doing there nor did they even care. I ended up leaving there. I caught a bus and was riding on the bus sobbing in my seat. As passengers were boarding and un-boarding, they would pass me up while I was sobbing. Some of the passengers tried to comfort me but I just could not respond, and I was unable to even talk. Finally, the driver asked me to leave the bus. When I left the bus, I noticed I was barefooted and then came to realize that it was not important for me to have shoes. Somehow, I ended up at the hospital and they were asking me about next of kin. All I had was my one sister in the next town, my oldest son three hours away, and my youngest over 1000 miles away in Florida, and I could not remember any of their phone numbers. I woke up to some kind of robotic sound only to find out it was my pill minder. When I woke up, I had an overwhelming feeling of weakness in my legs and arms, tears running down my eyes and a deep sense of sadness within me.

I have been going through all of Ron's ham radio equipment and getting them ready to sell. It's so hard going through his stuff. I had so many questions about his ham equipment, but he wasn't there to answer the questions. Watching this stuff go seems so finalizing.

I also went through my jewelry. He used to love to buy me pretty rings with gems and I loved receiving the jewelry from him, but these days the excitement of having the jewelry is gone and empty. They just no longer have the special value I held for them.

So many emotions. My anger is directed at the fact that he has not pushed himself to take care of himself. Smoking continued to be a habit. By now, he had swapped his preferred alcohol for wine and consumed at least five liters of alcohol per day. In addition to refusing an examination of his pacemaker, he refused to exercise.

As a result of my inability to convince him, I felt guilty about not getting him to stop smoking, drinking, exercising, and visiting the doctor. My disappointment came from the fact that I began to think I was his enabler. It is possible that I didn't express enough love towards him to make him feel as loved as he made me feel. Or maybe I didn't make him feel as needed as he made me feel needed.

My heart pounded. In what way will I be able to survive financially? Who will help me with my memory? It seems like I'm always forgetting things. Whenever I needed something to remind me of, he was there for me. I felt extremely lonely. All I have is two long-distance sons whom I do not see too often. I wish I had someone to do things with. or someone to talk to at any given

moment. Someone to share my thoughts and fears...
someone to give me confidence and compliments and
yes, I miss someone to argue with. I wanted what I lost.
I am fortunate to have many wonderful friends, but it
is that 24-hour 7 days week one-on-one thing that I am
missing. My childhood sweetheart is gone. My soulmate
is gone. My teacher is gone...My lover is gone, and My
sparring partner is gone. I have never lived alone. Always
have had human contact living with me. I Never had any
other man in my life, nor did I plan on another man. It
would have been next to impossible for another man to
fill Ron's shoes. I am sure in time out of mutual survival,
I will meet up with someone to go to dinner with and
possibly share some of my life with. No one will ever have
the entrance door opened like Ron had with me.

Something as simple as putting on my Linde star
pendant necklace breaks my heart because he used to
fasten it on my neck for me.

Finally, after much thought, I decided to reinvent
myself as a single woman. This was the first time in my
entire life that I lived alone. I lived with my mother until I
was 1 month from being 18 when we got married in 1964.

My first decision was to become a snowbird and
travel back and forth from Ohio in the winter to Florida
to visit my youngest son and then return to Ohio in
the summer to spend time with my oldest son. For the

summer months, I joined a health fitness club that was open 24/7. Then I got my passport thinking perhaps someday I would travel out of the country. I reinitiated my part-time quality control field representative job and my notary public activity so that I had extra income.

Just over 2 months after his passing, I started my first workout at the gym. As I was doing my workout, I was thinking of him. Wondering if he sees me. I knew if he saw me, he'd be proud of how I was standing up to the plate and taking this lonely task head-on. One night while I was working out, I lost my composure and broke down in tears. It's so hard and lonely.

I launched the boat into the water and docked it at the yacht club about 2 months before my husband passed away. After he passed away, it was a horrible feeling to go to the boat and see it knowing that my husband never had a chance to get in the boat. It was difficult. Weeks went by and I would go to the dock only to turn around and go home crying my eyes out. Finally, one day my friend Celeste talked to me to encourage me to take that boat out. She reminded me of my promise to her to take her out fishing that summer and she kept reminding me how my husband wanted me to enjoy that boat. I eventually took the boat out and every time I went out on the lake, I felt that his spirit was there with me. Every time we took the boat out, I would have a seagull follow the stern of my boat. When I anchored to fish, the seagull would just float behind my boat. Celesta was on the boat many times and got to the point when she would see the lonely seagull by our boat, she would say "Hi Ron, we are enjoying the boat" She truly believed it was Ron in that seagull. Fishing was prime, catching our limit of Perch and Walleye. I had plenty of fish to share with everyone,

I spent plenty of time at the dock with my boat, and then one day while I was at the dock cleaning my boat at the yacht club the yacht club manager approached me and asked me to run for the Rear Commodore position at the Yacht Club. Gosh, I had no idea what that was or what kind of duties it entailed. The manager's name was Bobbie. He explained to me about the position. He said it was easy and just a social thing so I accepted the nomination and won the election. To my surprise, being the Rear Commodore at the Yacht Club was intense and kept me quite busy. I met all kinds of people from all walks of life. I would participate in or conduct all kinds of events like Fish Fry, Spaghetti dinners, and sailboat racing. Sailboat racing was my favorite event.

Approximately 2 months after Ron's death I decided to have a dock party. It wasn't a good times party; it was merely a gathering of friends. I did not realize that it looked like I was celebrating him being gone as someone had suggested to me. I was just simply trying to move on and circle myself with friends to ease the pain. Ron was not big on social events. That was my department but now that I look back, I can see where someone would have misunderstood the purpose of the gathering. But it was not a wild party,

It was just a simple nice get-together with hotdogs, etc., and everyone had to bring a cover dish. This is when I first met Rita. She came to my gathering with a dish and introduced herself. She told me how much she enjoyed fishing. We became very good friends and went out fishing on the boat every chance we could. She helped clean the boat with each trip. Now I had Celesta and Rita as co-captains.

I hardly stayed home. I usually had breakfast and dinner out with friends I never went on so-called dates. Some people suggested that some of my outings with men were dates, but they were not dates of an affectionate nature. They were just friends. I never considered these outings as dates.

Snowbird

At the end of 2015, I took my first snowbird trip to Florida. I will always remember that long drive from Ohio to Florida. I sobbed on and off during that lonely trip. I felt pain in my heart. There were times when I was crying so hard, that I had to pull off because my sight was blurred from the tears. When I got to my son Ed's house my eyes were swollen from crying and he grabbed me and gave me the biggest hug. This is the first time I have seen him in four years so we both mourned the loss of Ron. He took me to my room where he and his girlfriend Liz set it up. The first thing I did was walk to the beach alone while Ed was at work.

On my first trip to Florida, I met up with Kim and her boyfriend who had flown in from Ohio for vacation and to see their 82-year-old grandmother Wanda. We met at the beach, and I was introduced to her Wanda.

Since that day, Wanda and I became close friends and did all kinds of things during my stay in Florida. We did a lot of dancing, went to the beaches, ate out almost daily and we took several road trips in Florida.

One day in September 2016, I thought I would hang out on my boat. Upon arriving at the marina, I discovered this huge sailboat docked across the river from my dock. It looked like a big Pirate Ship. My first thought was I sure wish Ron could see this. This boat changed my day. I ran over to the boat and while they were tying the boat up to the dock I welcomed them to our port. The boat was the Niagara out of PA. The crew was sailing Lake Erie and stopped in Black River to get supplies and fuel… I offered to take the cook to Giant Eagle for their supplies and they accepted the offer. Over $700 in groceries in my car to the boat. It certainly was ravenous crew. The cook was a cute little girl named Rosie with red hair and pigtails. I can only guess she was an Irish girl. After the shopping trip, they took me for a tour of this huge ship. 198 ft long...I was amazed at their galley. They used wood to cook. I could not believe how small and crowded the sleeping area was. This sure was an interesting tour.

After dealing with the crew on the Niagara, I went home to change clothes and then returned to my dock. The sailboat owner 2 docks away from me invited my friend Wendy and me to take a sailboat ride on the

Copasetic. I accepted the invitation while at the same time feeling like I might be doing something wrong sailing with another man even though it was just a neighborly thing. Everything turned out to be perfect on that day and night!! The first time I went sailing was at the age of seven with my aunt and uncle in Atlantic City.

It was my first sailboat ride as an adult. It was beautiful and peaceful, but during the entire trip, I was surely wishing my childhood sweetheart was there to enjoy it with me. I could almost feel his arm around my shoulder as we glided through the waters in the night.

I have been doing my workouts at the gym every other day. I would usually go anywhere between 3:30 and 6:00 in the morning because I didn't sleep well at night.

I contacted a support group of widows and joined them on a field trip to a local casino. The one woman who paired up with me has been widowed for 12 years. Her name was Jill. She said she still cries for her husband. I didn't want to do that. I didn't want to spend the rest of my life alone and crying for my husband. What do I do at 69 years old?

I continued my workouts and my Rear Commodore duties. I kept quite busy. Went fishing out on my boat every chance I could. I always had someone on the boat with me. Rita and Celesta would take turns going with me, but on occasions, they would come together. We always caught our legal limit of fish and the seagulls continued to follow us.

Our yacht club was hosting a perch fish fry event. Fish has been donated to the cause by several anglers, including myself. There was also other food provided by other members, such as potato salad and bakery items. Some of the proceeds went towards remodeling the Club House. My newfound friend Jill wanted to attend this event but did not want to drive at night so I told her she could spend the night at my house. In the morning, she asked me if she could stay at the house while I went to the yacht club to prepare for the event and I would pick her up in the afternoon to attend the event. She did. She left the event and went home. When I went home, I discovered my wedding rings along with special rings that Ron had made for me were missing. She took them and there was no one else that had access to my house. I made a police report on it, but it didn't do any good because she denied it and I didn't have proof that she took it. I was just crushed over this.

In 2017 during the first social event of the year at the yacht club, I met some members who had pilot licenses and invited me to a cookout at the local airport. I took them up on the offer to attend the cookout at the airport. At first, I was there just to be sociable and to make new friends but as it turned out, I developed a desire to fly.

Some of the pilots there were in their 70s. One of the pilots had his pilot license only about a year and he was 69 years old I thought wow… he is older than me and he can fly. I became intrigued with the idea of flying. One of my biggest fears at the time was flying. What better way to conquer fear?

I enrolled in a Pilot school to become a pilot. My thinking was that it would be a nice trip to fly to Florida every fall and back home in the spring. I knew my sons would be proud of my accomplishments. I will never forget my first flight in Piper Cub. I had the plane elevating upward toward the beautiful clouds. They looked like giant marshmallows. Then my instructor had me bank the plane so that we had a nice view of Lake Erie. At that moment, my love for flying was in full swing. I enjoyed flying as much as being captain of my boat and fishing!!

I continued to have problems getting a good night's sleep since the day my husband passed. I would wake up between 3 and 6 in the morning in the morning and go to the gym to work out. The world was asleep at that time After my one-hour workout, I would go home and get a couple of hours of sleep. Wake up way early in the morning and go to a medical health facility to get some swimming in. If the weather was permitting after my swim, I would go out fishing on the boat with my friend Celesta or Rita. After fishing, I would spend the afternoon with my flight lessons. One night during my waking hours I signed up with an online dating site Plenty of Fish in hopes of finding an elderly partner to enjoy company with. This was my first contact with Rich. He indicated in our online discussion that he was looking for a permanent relationship. I declined the offer and that was the end of Plenty of Fish for a while. In the meantime, I had acquired many friends and was successful as a snowbird where I would travel to Florida every winter.

It was common for me to attend social clubs such as the VFW and the American Legion to listen to the bands while I was in Ohio. I noticed this girl was dancing by herself. The fact that she was always by herself struck me as odd. In my introduction to her, I discovered that her husband had thrown her out of the house because he brought in another woman. Consequently, she is homeless and spending nights at her sister's house. Her name is Judy. As for her other home, she has it rented out and is moving into it in a few months when the lease expires. My heart went out to her as I felt her pain.

Her sole desire was to be a good wife for him and love him very much. As a last resort, I suggested to her that she use my spare bedroom until she could get a place. There are rules I set... You cannot have men in the house, you may not receive mail here, and you may not pay rent here. It was not my intention for her to consider it her home.

I just wanted to be of assistance to her. It all worked out well. She moved in with her tenants when they moved out, and we remain friends.

One of my previous co-workers stopped by the dock to introduce me to a musician named Sam. He needed some computer help with his recording equipment. Sam was fascinated with the things I did at my age. He wrote a song about me and titled it "FROM THE TIDES TO THE SKIES". I was so busy coming and going night and day that one of my neighbors told me that he thought I had become a "woman in the night" He was so wrong. He couldn't become further from the truth, I simply kept myself busy to save my mind.

I did my first flight in 2017 in Lorain Ohio. First time in an airplane and my first time flying and being hands-on at the controls of a plane. We flew to Port Clinton Ohio for lunch on my first trip. I experienced a piper cub and a Cessna. The game plan was to get my solo and nighttime flying hours in by flying from St. Petersburg Florida to Key West Florida. Then I would be able to fly solo. I even took 2 coolers of Perch and Walleye to Florida with me that year with plans to have a cookout with the St Petersburg pilots. I planned on introducing myself to the pilots by having a huge fish fry either at the airport or at my son's house in Florida. My fishing trips became more frequent and longer so that I could stockpile my fish for the cookout.

Towards the end of the season when I was getting a flying lesson the instructor told me to do a flyover at my home. I had a very difficult time finding my house I just couldn't pinpoint my home. Then one day I had my boat out on Lake Erie and when I came to shore, I had difficulty finding my port. I could not recognize the channel, so I had to use the GPS to return. Come to find out I had cataracts which is why I was unable to pinpoint my home from the airplane and why I could not recognize the port channels from the boat.

Before leaving for my yearly trip to Florida in 2017 I had cataract surgery. My friend Rita accompanied me to drive to Florida in the fall of 2017 with all our fish for my Snowbird trip and continued with the plan of flying to Key West. I intended to go to Florida for the winter months to finish my flight requirements by flying from St Petersburg Florida to Key West. Florida. Both my sons and friends were excited about my flying adventure. My sons were exceptionally excited that they would be flying with me to Key West. We took all kinds of fish with us for the fish fry. Rita decided to accompany me on my trip to Florida because I just finished my cataract operation, and she would have a vacation. When we arrived, Rita and I did a Fish fry at Ed's house. Rita stayed in Florida for.

about 2 weeks, and we did all kinds of things together. We took two coolers full of fish with us to Florida and had a couple of fish fry In the spring of 2017. During the two-week stay in Florida, Rita and I did many road trips. We went to Cape Coral to visit one of her long-lost relatives, then to Key West.

Rita and I had a whirlwind of fun for those two weeks. After Rita left for Ohio, I started to have difficulty seeing in the sun. My son sent me to an eye doctor to find out I had a mini stroke. The doctor wanted me to admit myself to the hospital immediately, but I declined because I was committed that evening to meet up with friends arriving from Ohio for dinner. I knew if I went to the hospital at that moment, nothing would be done until morning so I promised him I would admit myself in the hospital first thing in the morning. I did as promise and signed myself in the hospital the next morning and had surgery to clean the carotid artery.

Fortunately, the stroke did minimal damage, however, with my age of 73 now approaching with a history of a stroke, I decided to scrap my pilot plans and just be glad I had the opportunity to experience piloting an airplane. The thought of having a stroke while flying a plane and crashing down to earth injuring or killing pedestrians was haunting to me. I recovered from the surgery and headed back to my home in Ohio.

Rita came to visit me in the spring of 2018 and helped me drive home. We enjoyed ourselves dancing and going to the beach and having dinners on the gulf shores. Shortly after returning home in the spring of 2018 from Florida, I had a nasty fall at home, broke my right shoulder, and displaced my left elbow. I tripped and flew into the corner of the kitchen hitting the cabinet so hard that a drawer opened, and my left arm slammed into that drawer and dangled from it. Immediately I lost control of that limb. I tried to lift the arm with my right hand, but I was so weak I fell onto my right shoulder with my nose down in the corner. At this point, I had no control over both arms. Being home alone, I realized I was in big trouble. I knew I had to do something. I was alone in the house and had no way to get help. I used my legs to help flip myself over onto my back where I was able to breathe easier. A few seconds had gone by and my friend Celesta who is a retired nurse just happened to stop over at that moment. She had a key to the house so that she could check on it while I was in Florida and occasionally check on me. When she found me on the floor in the kitchen, she knew I was in trouble She immediately called 911. While making the 911 call, she proceeded to use her nursing skills on me. When the paramedics arrived, they took over and took me to the hospital by ambulance where they kept me for some time. As soon as the ambulance got me to the emergency room, they took me into surgery. The first thing they did was put my elbow in place. It was displaced from the fall then they were going to give me a shoulder replacement but while prepping me for surgery, the doctor noticed the fresh incision in my carotid artery and decided against the operation because it was too risky with me recovering from a recent carotid operation, my age and my extremely high blood pressure. After a couple of weeks in the hospital, I was transferred to a rehab nursing home because I had no use of both my arms. My son from Ohio took a leave of absence from work because he wanted to take care of me, but I needed personal hygiene care and certainly did not want to burden my son Ron with something like that. How can a son physically help his mom go to the bathroom? To me, that was unacceptable and humiliating for both me and my son. When it came time for me to return home from the nursing home, I went online with Amazon and ordered a Bidet so that I could do my hygiene care on my own.

My grandson Chris moved into the downstairs apartment with his family, so I had someone at the house to help me. He would cut the grass and do maintenance around the house in exchange for rent. The family did not want me to live alone.

I struggled the entire 2018 year with the healing of my shoulder by taking the required physical therapy. Every single day was painful. I couldn't even fish much, but I continued the role of Rear Commodore.

With my arm in a cast, I was unable to safely take my boat on a fishing trip. I was not able to maneuver the boat to dock. Boating for this year was done. Ken, one of the yacht club members who also was an angler, approached me and offered to take me on his boat fishing since it was difficult for me to drive my boat with a cast on my arm and shoulder. He said all I had to do was keep his boat on course with my good hand while he and his friend Sonny trolled for Walleye. With another licensed person onboard the the limit of fish on the boat would be lifted and we can split the catch 3 ways. I accepted the offer and stocked my freezer up with fish again.

I spent almost the entire summer recovering from the shoulder. My boat was no longer enjoyable to me. I sat on it several times, disgusted that I was no longer able to enjoy it

The last event I attended on the water was as a commodore operating the Official Command boat during the Regatta's Sailboat Race. I invited my friend Maria on the Command boat with me. I thought it would be nice for her to participate since she has never seen a sailboat race let alone be part of one. Just as we got out to port, I set my anchor and gave the start signal to the sailboat racers. I noticed we were getting closer to the break wall.

Maria tried to stop the boat from hitting the wall with her legs. I grabbed one of the dock sticks and handed it to her and told her to use that because she might break her legs hitting that wall. In the meantime, I held against the wall with the other dock stick while sending out a mayday signal to the Coast Guard. The Coast Guard came and pulled us away from the wall. By holding our sticks against the wall stopping the boat from slamming and the quick response from the coast guard we prevented major damage to the boat, although there were a lot of scrapes on the side of the boat. After they pulled the boat away from the wall, I put the boat at the dock and realized I was done with the boat because I was no longer as strong as I used to be. I was very miserable that year. My range of motion with my arm was limited.

When it came time to return to Florida in the spring of 2019, I decided that I would take my boat to Florida with me because I thought my son in Florida would have better use for the boat. My thinking was that since I am limited on the use of my arm, then I would be limited on the use of the boat.

During one of the yacht club events, I was having a conversation with another yacht club member Scott, and his girlfriend Liz about my episode with my boat and how I was planning on taking the boat to Florida with me. He volunteered to help transport my boat to Florida. I took him up on his offer and he did most of the driving because I was still]wearing a shoulder brace. Scott was also a pilot.

On the trip to Florida hauling the boat, two axles broke on the boat trailer. They broke just as we entered Florida. Scott made sure to grease and examine the axles and tires before we left Ohio, but they still broke. My guess is because we went through some heavy road construction in Georgia. It was such a nightmare just to get someone to give us roadside assistance. We were approximately 200 miles from my son's house. We were stranded on the side of the road for six hours.

Finally, we arrived at my son's house without the boat because we had to leave the boat on the trailer at a repair shop until we got the parts. It took us a week to find the replacement axles and when we got it repaired, we brought it to my son's house. Ed (my son) set out to repair this boat and shined it up like new. Scott went about his business visiting some of his Floridian friends and then headed back home to Ohio.

As a follow-up to my artery surgery from the year before, I went to the doctor in Florida. After my fall, my artery was compromised, and I needed a stent. This leads to the installation of a stent.

Rita came to Florida, and we continued to socialize with friends. With the Constant shoulder pain, a stent in the carotid artery, and physical therapy from the shoulder, our trip to Florida was not that enjoyable. At this point, the weather was the only thing I enjoyed in Florida. We made the best of it with Florida road trips.

When the time came for me to return to Ohio, Rita drove my truck on my behalf to get me there. I made the most of my summer in Ohio after returning home. Constantly suffering from shoulder pain, a visit to the therapy pool visit was part of my daily routine. My pain was relieved while I was in the therapy pool.

Ed was going to take care of the boat when I returned home to Ohio, but when I left Florida, something came up and he was unable to pull the boat out of the water for maintenance. To solve the issue, I hired someone from Craigslist to get my boat out of the water and put it in storage. It was without my permission that the person I hired sold the boat. As a result, I was left without a boat. The guy insisted I send him the title repeatedly. Despite my persistent refusal to sell it, I was determined not to sign that title over.

In an attempt to get the title, the buyer kept harassing me over the phone. I was having no luck with these guys, so I reached out to the county sheriff in Ohio about this issue. While in their sheriff's office, the guy who bought the boat called me. I handed over the phone to the deputy to talk to this buyer. When the deputy spoke with him on the phone and told him that he had stolen goods and that he needed to return my boat. The deputy advised me to report the boat stolen in Florida. In Ohio that would have been classified as theft on receiving stolen goods. I returned to Florida and filed a stolen report, but the tables turned on me and I was charged with fraud for filing a false stolen report in Florida. Florida saw this issue as a bad deal between me and the guy I hired to put the boat in storage. The Florida prosecutor said the guy who bought the boat did not steal it because he paid money for it even though I made it clear to him that I did not want to sell the boat. The Attorney in Florida advised me to sign the title. At first, I declined to cooperate because it was my boat!! However, my Floridian Lawyer said that if I don't turn over the title, they will swear a warrant out for my arrest. Reluctantly I signed over the title and after my name I wrote signed in duress. After the title was transferred all charges were dropped and there were no police reports to be found, I was without a boat with bitter feelings and emotions. I did make one last call to that buyer. I told him, "You may brag to your family and friends that you bought a beautiful boat, so when you go out on the gulf with your family or friends, just remember, because of the way you acquired that boat doesn't mean its yours in spirit. It belongs to me because my deceased husband bought itfor me before he passed away. Just remember that" then I hung up the phone and never heard from him after that.

At the end of the year, I received a reverse shoulder replacement in my right shoulder followed by another stay in the nursing home for recovery. My son took care of me after the nursing home. Soon after my recovery from surgery, I returned to Florida and continued my physical therapy again in Florida. On this trip, my friend Rita drove down to Florida with me. We took a bunch of fish with us to Florida because Lake Erie perch was a treat to our friends in Florida. We had a perch fish fry with my son and our Floridian friends at his house.

Rita and I went on sightseeing road trips in Florida. I introduced Rita to some of my Florida friends including Wanda and Mary Jo. Wanda lived in St Petersburg Florida. We had another Perch fish fry at Wanda's house. I also introduced her to a recently acquired friend of mine by the name of Julie who also lived in St Petersburg Florida. Julie's husband was a former Minnesota Viking Football player. Julie was another place where we had a perch fish fry. They had a beautiful home on the intercoastal water with an in-ground swimming pool. Julie invited Rita and me to swim in her pool and we took her up on it. After about a week later Rita had to fly back home to Ohio. I finished the winter months in Florida and returned to Ohio in the fall.

While in Ohio in 2019, I continued my aquatic physical therapy daily. At the end of the year, I went to the orthopedic doctor and complained that the pain was horrific and we needed to take action. The pain became too much for me to bear, so the doctor sent me to the hospital so I could receive an injection. The doctor at the hospital took an x-ray to pinpoint the location of where to put the injection. As he looked at my shoulder, he was shocked to see that there was no connection between my arm and shoulder.

I immediately went to another orthopedic doctor to get a second opinion and it was decided that I had a huge amount of damage to my shoulder and arm and therefore needed to have a reverse shoulder operation. I was hospitalized for shoulder reversal surgery and spent recovery time in the nursing home and when I was done, I stayed at my son's house in Ohio until it was time to return to Florida.

A vacation was taken by Rita in the spring of 2020 when she drove my truck to Florida. She stayed for about a week. Since my surgery had just been performed, we just relaxed and enjoyed the scenery, beaches, and music.

Rita and I visited my friends Helena and Wanda in Florida. We had a good time going to the beaches and things like that. Rita, Wanda, and I went to Tampa to meet up and have lunch with one of my friends Helena. It was a nice visit.

In the days following Rita's departure, I began physical therapy for my shoulder. While sitting idle in Florida got on the dating site called Plenty of Fish. Being in a relationship was the last thing on my mind, and I just wanted to kill some time.

It was just a matter of wanting a friend. It would be nice to have someone who shares the same interests as me. On this dating site, I met a lot of guys online, but not in person, but not many appealed to me. This was my first contact with Rich. It was at that time that Rich wanted to meet with me, but I declined because I did not want to start a relationship with him, and he seemed to be seeking a long-term relationship with me. I just wanted to be in Florida to enjoy the weather with my Floridian friends and finish the therapy sessions.

At the end of Therapy sessions in Florida, the epidemic of COVID-19 erupted. Florida shut down!!! All beaches were closed. all entertainment in Florida was shut down, and Tiki bars closed!! The stores ran out of supplies and friends went into hibernation and quarantined themselves.

The governor of Florida issued a stay-at-home mandate threatening high fines if caught being out in public if it was unessential business. I tried to stay in quarantine in Florida, but it was too traumatizing for me.

Even playing around on a dating site was quite boring so I fled from Florida to my home in Ohio. I ran away from Florida and headed to Ohio thinking there was germ warfare going on. I drove 1000 miles non-stop except for fuel. I Drove my 2016 GMC Truck from Florida to Home with my arm in a sling, stopping only to refuel and go to the bathroom. My father's conversations with me came to mind while I was driving. I recalled in some of our conversations, that he told me that someday, the United States would be attacked. I remember how he used to tell me war stories when I was a child, and the idea of warfare has remained with me to this day. Chemicals or germs would be used in warfare, according to him. This is why I believed we were being attacked.

Upon arriving in Ohio, I discovered that Ohio was also shut down, there was no one to talk to because everyone hibernated in their homes putting themselves in quarantine and not even accepting visitors.

Simply by arriving from Florida where COVID-19 infection levels were high, I was automatically quarantined by law. Stores had limited supplies, and very few restaurants were open. Friends in Ohio also locked themselves in their homes.

In April of 2020, going on 74 years old… Feeling all alone, trying to beat boredom, I entertained myself by going back online to the dating site. Again, I started communicating with Rich on plenty of fish. I decided to amuse myself and do the unthinkable. Focus on the dating site!! This is when I connected with Rich. I have always told my friends not to go on dating sites because it could be dangerous. I also expressed to my friends never to meet a guy alone let alone in the dark or an out-of-the-way place.

After a few telephone and text conversations, it seemed that we had moved on to another level and decided to meet up despite the quarantine.

Rich was the caretaker for a campground during the winter and the first meetup was at the campground. I don't know what I was thinking... because it was wintertime at the campground, and no one was around. Despite my advice to my friends about such a dangerous move, I went ahead and met with him at his campground. Maybe I did this because I thought in my mind that we were under some sort of germ warfare or something. I thought it was going to be the end of the world and did not want to be by myself. Rich invited me over for a cup of coffee. Reluctantly against my judgment, I decided to go meet this guy in person by myself that evening in the dark at a campground that was closed for the season. I made sure to pack my gun in the truck and wore comfortable clothing so that I could run if need be. As I pulled up to his camper, he was standing outside to greet me. He did not appear as a man who was financially well off. My first thought was oh boy, we are in germ warfare, and I am meeting up with a drunk. Oh well, it's not like I don't know how to handle drunks. There is no one else to socialize with. My father and husband were alcoholics so I am sure I can handle this one. As it turns out, I was completely wrong on this. He has never drunk alcohol or smoked. I found it hard to believe that this man was a professional softball player, a Vietnam veteran, a gambler, and never drank or smoked. But it worked out ok after meeting several times, we both realized we both had a lot in common. As we conversed about our past, we realized there were times when we were younger, that we could have met up and not realized it. There are so many things we have in common. It is no wonder we didn't connect way.

We knew there was no danger to either of us upon meeting each other. I had numerous self-defense training and packing a gun and I was not about to be harmed by this man Both of us were avid anglers, and loved animals, nature, gambling, traveling, and the challenge of playing games, especially card games, He loved reading and I loved writing. I told him about some of the books I wrote and how I started to write another one when my husband passed. Rich tried to encourage me to continue writing the book.

New Beginning

I lost my husband of 51 years in 2015 Rich lost his wife in 2012. We were two individuals who knew nothing about each other, We no longer had anyone to share our life with and we both with a lot of private praying, continued to just survive living without a purpose until we met each other.

Rich is a Vietnam veteran was retired from the post office and has had a colonoscopy bag since 1996 caused by Crohn's disease. He had a pacemaker inserted in 2017. Although he had health problems, he still maintained his life alone starting at age 69 after his wife passed. He took up residency in a campground as a caretaker during both closed seasons and the busy season. Besides reading, watching TV, socializing with other campers, and keeping up with sports, he engaged in a variety of other activities. Following the advice of a couple of camping friends, he joined the online dating site Plenty of Fish.

I have been a Notary Public for the state of Ohio since 1969 but my primary career was as a computer systems manager until 2002. I was diagnosed with LUPUS in 2002 which caused me to take an early retirement from my primary job in 2008. I kept my notary public commission and part-time with the quality control company. They would call on me from time to time for a field assignment.

My favorite pastimes were cooking, gardening, and fishing. I used to love to go to Lake Erie and catch those perch and walleye. I have been told Lake Erie is the Walleye capital of the world.

I was 69 years old when my husband passed away in 2015. I can recall after his death I felt this emptiness within me and all around and even though I had friends and family trying to smother me, I felt alone. Married for 51 years and suddenly the world stopped. The world was full of people, and yet it felt empty. No one to wake up to, No one to share thoughts with. Now I have no chores to do, no cooking to do, no cleaning to do, and no caring to do. Even though some of these activities can be annoying, without them there seems to be no point in life!!

I have two sons, one of whom lives over 200 miles away and the other who lives over 1500 miles away. I was alone and my mind would race especially during the night hours. Up to this point, my husband and children have occupied all of my time and attention over the years

Except for my husband, I have never had an intimate relationship with anyone else. Over the course of the last 51 years, I have devoted every minute to my husband and children. In a flash, it has become my time instead of theirs.

Rich and I spent our COVID-19 epidemic time taking road trips in my truck and cruising along the western shores of Lake Erie. We would play music during our trips. I was impressed that Rich knew most of the song titles and the artist. One of the trips in the beginning there was a song by George Jones called "WALK THROUGH THIS WORLD WITH ME". We both related to that song. To this day that song remains to be a special song for us.

Port Clinton, Catawba, Marblehead, Vermillion, Huron, Lorain, and others were among the lighthouses we saw on the western side of Lake Erie. During our visits to the western shores of Lake Erie, we received our National Park Card.

On one of our trips, we visited Johnson's Island located on the shores of Lake Erie in Sandusky Bay. I have been fishing up and down these shores all my life and never knew this place existed. It was at this island where we checked out the Confederate cemetery. It was the site of a prisoner-of-war camp of captured Confederate officers and soldiers from the Civil War. A few pictures were taken under the Confederate monument with Rich and me. A detailed historical discussion of the events that this place was associated with was narrated by Rich. As a result of our fascination with this island, we visited it twice. On our second visit, we took my friend Debbie with us to see this island.

Although many places were closed due to the COVID-19 outbreak, we still took road trips and photographed these beautiful, majestic lighthouses!

We also visited the African Safari right outside of Port Clinton and the Catawba Islands. We had a Buffalo and Camel tried to get in the car window. As part of another road trip, we went to Sandusky Ohio, and took the ferry over to Put N Bay for lunch. As we traveled along the west coast of Lake Erie, we checked out every lighthouse we passed.

I maintained my Notary Public Commission since 1969, and occasionally performed field service assignments, though both of us were on a fixed income.

Keeping my commission active was a good thing because the COVID-19 epidemic resulted in a boom in Notary business. The bank closings had created a huge demand for Notaries.

We both contracted COVID-19. I was the first to catch it. I think I may have contracted COVID-19 at charity auction that the police department was having.

In addition to being unable to breathe, we were very

weak with symptoms of pneumonia. Rich took good care of me and I was very impressed with Rich's nursing skills He then became very ill with COVID-19 just as I was recovering. As a means of forcing the lungs to work, I used a breathing spirometer on both of us. When Rich got sick, I was very concerned for him. There was a spike in his temperature of 102 degrees. As a precaution, I would give him Tylenol and monitor his oxygen levels. We were sick for about 2 weeks.

After I had COVID I was not able to smell or taste anything. To this day, I don't smell or taste things as good as I did before. Rich ended up deaf from it.

I took advantage of my Notary skills and took on side jobs to help pay for our travels. Our first road trip after recovering from COVID-19 we returned to Put N Bay Island to do a Notary assignment. While in Put N Bay, we had Lunch.

In one of our discussions I told Rich about my loss of the boat. He was very sympathetic to what had happened and decided to buy a boat because I remained disturbed by the incident at the fact that I lost my boat. The fact that my boat was taken from me rather than giving it up willingly did not sit well with me. Rich was determined to find a boat for us and ambitiously shopped for the perfect boat and finally in 2020 we found one in Michigan. Another road trip and the boat were purchased.

Until April 2020, we stored the boat in my yard. The boat was checked out at the lake by Rich and my grandson Chris, who made sure it floated and worked properly. A test fishing trip on Lake Erie was then scheduled for June. We launched the boat into Lake Erie with my friend Rita. It was a beautiful day out on the lake.

The three of us had a beautiful relaxing day on the water. At the end of the trip, Rich had taken the boat out of the water, as we were preparing the boat to be trailered back to the house, Rita climbed up the back of the boat to check the engine lift. After she climbed up the swim ladder at the back of the boat, the ladder broke just as she reached the top of the boat's stern, and it propelled her onto me.

My mind still vividly recalls lying on the ground and Rich telling me the ambulance was coming. As I remember seeing my hand full of blood and the world spinning around me, I felt like I was dying. Of all things to have an accident like this during COVID. The fall was on cement and left me with a concussion and a broken shattered leg. It left Rita with a sprained elbow.

Again, I ended up in serious condition in the hospital. This time I was only permitted to have one visitor because of the COVID epidemic. I had to decide who to choose to visit me. My Ohio son lived 200 miles away, and the other one lived in Florida, so that wasn't an option. Rita was with us, but she had a family to tend to so the only person left was Rich. He was at my side the entire time in the hospital.

Rich took very good care of me. I did not have to go to rehab this time because Rich stood up to the plate and volunteered to be my caretaker. The physical therapist came to the house but was unable to do the actual therapy that needed to be done because the right shoulder was nonbearing meaning was unable to use crutches or a walker due to my right shoulder recovering from an operation and still in a sling.

Rich and my friends arranged to get an electric wheelchair, a manual wheelchair for outdoor use, and a walker. Rich and my older son Ron met each other for the first time while I was in the hospital. It is not the way I would have liked my boyfriend to meet my son. They teamed up and built a handicap ramp for me at the house while I was in the hospital.

Our road trips got a little complicated, but we still did them. Now there were walkers and wheelchairs involved. He would push me all over with the wheelchair. We continued many road trips...and even took me to the casinos We would go grocery shopping. He would put a shopping cart in front of my wheelchair so I could grasp the shopping cart handle and stir the carts while he would push my wheelchair like a train, and this is how we shopped for quite a while.

Complications with my shoulder suddenly set in with an infection into the implants in my shoulder which required me to get surgery to remove the implants. I wondered if COVID-19 caused this infection. While waiting for my appointment day, Rich became ill and ended up hospitalized with pancreatitis and a gall bladder attack. He had to be hospitalized to get his gallbladder removed. While Rich was in the hospital, I had to keep my appointment to have the surgery done to remove the implants in my shoulder due to an infection. We were hospitalized 200 miles apart. When Rich was discharged from the hospital, Rich's daughter Tina picked Rich up and had him stay with her for a few days until I was back at home. The hospital released me with a PICC line inserted into my heart. A PICC line was a long thin tube that was inserted through a vein in my arm and passed through the larger vein near the heart. The therapy was prescribed for 6 weeks. Rich's daughter Tina brought Rich home when I came back from the hospital. We had visiting nurses coming to check on us and one of the nurses educated my son Ron on dispensing the antibiotic through the PICC line. He was so nervous that he shook every time. The whole experience was overwhelming to him, and he had a difficult time doing this to his mother. My son tried to overcome his uncomfortable feelings until he ended up having a stroke because of his efforts. He had to leave to take care of his medical issues, so Rich finished the intravenous injections of the antibiotics for about 2 weeks. The stroke left my son without the use of his right arm.

Rich and I had many discussions on traveling and came up with a plan to do a long road trip traveling from Ohio to Florida, then across the southern states turning up to Nevada, and then return home to Ohio for the winter. With all this discussion. We decided that it would be a good idea to purchase a camper to travel with. Rich searched for a camper the way he did for the boat. We had a routine where Rich would go inside the prospective camper with his cell phone and video chat with me so I could see inside the unit because after all, I was still in a wheelchair unable to climb the steps into the campers. Finally, a camper was purchased and travels with the camper began. Several trips with the camper to various casinos from Michigan to the Pocono mountains. We went west to Michigan to hit the casinos. When we were done with the Michigan Casino, our friends Judy and Dennis went with us to camp at Toby Hannah State Park in Pennsylvania. While we were set up in camp, we took advantage of the moment and visited the beautiful Mount Airy Casino. Both places were beautiful.

We stopped off at Norristown Pennsylvania and visited with Rich's ex-softball coach and friend Sonny.

These trips occupied most of our summertime. By this time, I was out of the wheelchair, but still had my leg wrapped and supported.

Summer ended and my leg support was not needed as much, so we began to get ready for our Road trip to the south and west.

Florida Homestead

It was time for that cross-country travel!! So as planned we Traveled to Florida in 2021. We stopped over in Central Florida to visit the Sibert family. I have known them for over 60 years. I met Joyce and Russ in 1962 on a double date when I was a teenager with my late husband Ron. As time went by, I boarded some horses in Joyce's barn until my oldest son was two years old. Joyce's daughters Linda, and Shirley, and Shirley's husband Jerry allowed us to set up our camper in their drive. While there, we played cards with them almost nightly and had many dinners. They were very kind to me and Rich. While visiting with my friends, I became ill and Rich took me to the emergency room because I developed severe pain and swelling in the injured leg. The diagnosis was excessive stress on that leg. Having had surgery on my leg, the doctor advised me to avoid travel since sitting in the car for long periods could cause a blood clot.

So that plan for traveling across the country was canceled. In the meantime, I did aquatic physical therapy for the leg.

We were in Florida only for a couple of weeks when Rich's dog started getting very weak and could hardly stand up. She was 24 years old. She would wobble when she walked and sometimes would just fall. Rich did not want to see her suffer anymore so he had her put to sleep and had her cremated. We have her ashes buried on our land

In 2021 Rita came out to visit us while we were at our friend's house. Rich's son and family came to Florida to get married. Rita and Wanda joined us to attend Rich's son's wedding on St Pete's beach. The weather was perfect for a wedding on the beach.

We took frequent road trips to St Petersburg to fish on the infamous Sunshine Skyway Bridge Pier and of course stop at Skyway Jack's for an awesome breakfast. On one occasion on the way to St Petersburg, I saw the boat that was taken from me. It was in a field, and it looked like it was damaged pretty bad. I did hope no one was hurt from it but at the same time, I was thinking Karma prevailed.

We always had a great time on the pier of the Sunshine Skyway bridge. It was exciting to see the dolphins trying to steal our bait. One time Rich helped rescue a pelican that had was wrapped up in fishing string with a hooked lure in his beak.

Russ passed away in 2022 and Joyce followed in 2023. I am blessed to have spent some time with my long-time friends before they passed on. Her Children treated us like family. I did a lot of physical therapy in their pool. Shirley and Jerry went out of their way to convert us to Floridian residents. Shirley kept bringing an available property to our attention until we finally found a piece of land and bought it.

Rich and I had discussions about getting a place in Florida for a summer home. Shirley found us a piece of property for sale in Florida. It was a half-acre piece of land located in a little town called Old Town along the Suwannee River with a dilapidated mobile home. We purchased it and decided that I would sell my home in Ohio. The plan was to live in the camper while we renovated the dilapidated mobile home which was 8 ft wide and 42 ft long.

I Sold Elyria's home in Feb 2022 and moved everything to Florida with a giant UHall truck. The move was stressful!! I resigned from my Ohio Notary Commission and acquired the Florida Notary Commission. My little field representative job and the Notary Business helped offset travel expenses and mobile home renovations. We lived in the Camper while the home was being remodeled. Now the mobile home is 24' X 42' instead of 8' X 42'. We converted the mobile home to a ranch house.

Rich did most of it with the help of various laborers in the area. In 2023 the remodeling was completed enough to move into it. Every wall and floor was replaced except the front exterior wall, but the interior part was replaced.

Right from the first day of residency on the property, we noticed multiple cardinals. Males and females. Almost as if they were pets. They fly all around us and they remain in the area to this day. I have read According to a poem, "Cardinals appear when Angels are near," many people believe that seeing a red cardinal near their home is a sign of comfort and guidance from an angel, and a reminder to embrace new beginnings. Some also believe that cardinals are messengers from the spiritual realm, symbolizing hope, vitality, and the presence of loved ones who have passed away. I like to believe that our loved ones are the angels watching over us.

In 2022 Hurricane Ian hit Florida. This was our first experience with a hurricane. We didn't know if our do-it-yourself renovated home would withstand the hurricane, so Rich and I decided to do a road trip to the North. We went to Georgia, then to a casino in Alabama. After we spent some time at the casino in Alabama, we went to Mississippi. We enjoyed the casinos and did some sightseeing. By then Hurricane Ian left Florida so we made our way down to the gulf shores and headed to our Florida home. On the way, we stopped in Louisiana to visit their casinos and drove to the northern Gulf Coast to return home. Upon returning home we were thrilled that there was no damage at our home. Some tree limbs fell in the field and driveway. Of course, there was lots of damage in other areas of Florida, but we were fortunate to withstand the storm.

We made the best of it while the home was being renovated by going to all kinds of places to explore Florida. We went to just about every restaurant in a tri-county area. One of the restaurants was a down-home Dixie-style buffet. Great homemade food and another restaurant was right on the Suwannee River. In a little town off the Gulf along the Suwannee River was a restaurant where one would think it is condemned. All the wood outside seemed to be dull and washed out. When entering this restaurant, I was surprised at how clean the interior was. Everything had a shine to it and the food was fantastic. There is another restaurant that has all kinds of buffet foods. Mostly oriental food. One time Rich saw an ad about a restaurant located in a private campground and decided to take me there for a surprise. It turned out to be a sports bar with a younger crowd around 40 years younger than us. Most of the girls were half dressed and the place was very loud. The waitress had a hard time hearing us for our order.

Dining out was not the only adventure we had. We went to many events. One event was a real horse rodeo with real cowboys and cowgirls. I have never been to a rodeo. We would never know ahead of time what adventure we would do for the day. We have seen many exotic animals like Camels, zebras, and Kangaroos because these types of animals can survive in Florida. There are numerous animal sanctuaries throughout the state.

We have been on several fishing charter boat trips in St Petersburg, Tarpon Springs, and Cedar Key Florida. We would catch our limit of fish and go to Shirley's and Jerry's house to do a fish fry. Other times we would fish on shore in Cedar Key.

Gambling is in both our blood so of course we tried our gambling skills on casino boats. One in Cape Canaveral and the other one in Port Ritchey and then the casino in Tampa.

It was an all-day event whenever we went someplace The doctor's offices are at least 50 miles away.

Of course, we continued to build our home between road trips. Most of the work was done by Rich. We tried to hire locals and many times it was a nightmare because people lied claiming they had experience, but they did not. It was a very trying time getting this project completed. One of the contractors we hired was robbing us of our personal belongings. Another contractor was ordering excessive building supplies and taking them home. None of them did professional work.

Rich's daughter Tina arrived in Orlando with her family for a vacation and invited us to spend a week with them We did, and it was a very nice time.

In the fall of 2023, Rich parked the truck in front of the grocery store to help me in the truck and return the handicap scooter basket. While he was returning the basket another truck hit our truck broadside and totaled it. Rich and the driver of the truck that hit me were concerned that I may have been injured because it was a hard hit. But how can I say I was injured from the truck hitting me when I was already in a sling from my fall? Even though the accident was not our fault the insurance rates jumped considerably high, and I had to get a new truck leaving me with a truck payment. The officer that was called to the scene wrote on his report that we were both at fault because the other driver lost control of his vehicle and our vehicle was parked in a no parking zone. The officer did not realize that I was handicapped and that I did have a handicap plate and therefore that is an exception to parking there because Rich was unloading me. Consequently, my auto insurance was increased.

It was difficult to find help to rebuild the mobile home. Everything was done with cash and credit cards.

I raised my credit card bill and lowered my credit score, but the home was completed!!! We built our own home together. We probably spent three times the money than we should of because we had to keep redoing shabby work

Later in 2023, Rich's other daughter Beth from Ohio came with her two daughters, son, and husband to visit us just as Hurricane Idalia hit our area. All the events I had planned for them were canceled due to the hurricane. Our friend Jerry invited us to come stay in his big brick home in Fort White for the hurricane. We had a hurricane party and had a lot of fun there. It was Beth and her family's first time in a hurricane. We played cards and just enjoyed quality time with the kids. Most places remained closed after the hurricane went through, however, there were some nice restaurants open that we took them to. We also took them to the Everglades. We all had a great time at the Everglades, and each had the opportunity to hold a baby alligator. They loved it there.

On the way back from the Everglades, Rich had heart attack symptoms and was hospitalized in a hospital in Naples Florida for a week Rich's family had to reluctantly leave him to return to Ohio because they had to report to work. The outcome of that hospitalization was that Rich was suffering from an acute pancreatitis attack.

Growth in Florida

We purchased another piece of property that was attached to our land. That increased our property size from half an acre to one acre. The property was dense with Floridian weeds and Trees. Too much for Rich and me to handle and reliable help was scarce, so we decided to get a goat to help clear their property.

A billy goat was adopted by us. It was Rich who named him Butthead. It wasn't long before we realized Buthead was lonely in that pasture, so we decided to go get another goat to keep him company. We visited a goat farm and ended up buying another goat and named her Miss Daisy. However, during the visit to purchase Miss Daisy, I noticed two tiny goats. One was blue and the other was brown. They looked like stuffed toys. They were so young they wobbled as they walked. Oh my, they were like overloaded with cuteness. I fell in love with the baby blue goat. This tiny goat came running into the field with its brown-colored twin. Rich put that goat on order to purchase when it became available at 3 months old.

After 3 months passed, we went to pick up the cute little blue goat and ended up getting both of them. We named the blue goat Blue and the Brown goat Brownie. Upon arriving home with our new goats there was a big dog in the pasture chasing the other two goats. It turned out to be a neighbor dog harassing our goats, so we decided to get a pair of African geese for the pasture. We named them Hanzel and Gretel. They do a great job guarding the property. In the meantime, a rooster strolled into the field and became a member of our property. He made his home in a tree. Rich calls him Rascal.

By now we started having problems with the goats escaping. Such escape artists!! So we installed an electric fence. We purchased a solar fence charger and hired a local laborer to run the wire for us. It works great.

Several months pass by and the goats no longer escape, and no dogs are harassing the goats. It seems that the electric fence keeps our kids in and the geese keep the dogs out. Problems are solved and we feel confident that our animals are safe. We noticed the geese had laid eggs and Miss Daisy looked like she was expecting.

We reserved a cruise to the Bahamas for2the spring of 2024, so we took a cruise to the Bahamas. Unfortunately,

I was ill with diverticulitis for the first time in my life. I was unable to do anything on that ship. I didn't even go off the ship at the ports because I was so miserable. I was sure this was the end for me. I thought I was dying from cancer or something. I didn't know I had this condition until I returned home and went to the doctor. But Rich stood by my side and stayed with me. I tried to get Rich to go about his business and enjoy the cruise. I wanted him to go to the shows and go sightseeing at the ports without me. I wanted him to enjoy himself and not let me be a burden to him but he stayed right at my side proclaiming that it was his job. He made cosure I was always kept warm. It seemed all I could do was sleep. We had a great room overlooking the water. The water view was very relaxing for me. After we returned home Rich took me to the emergency room because I started vomiting uncontrollably. I was extremely sick. My blood pressure was extremely high at 200/109. I was tested for COVID-19 and it was negative. The hospital staff managed to get my blood pressure down and got fluids in me with an IV. They said I was dehydrated. A few days later I followed up with my doctor and he did a CAT scan of my chest, stomach, and pelvis. That's when he diagnosed me with diverticulitis. I have heard of this sickness before and even a couple of my friends had this. Now I know what they went through. NOT PRETTY! I promised Rich that we would go on another cruise when we could enjoy it.

There is plenty to do in Florida. We both love and enjoy animals, especially horses. We attend rodeos often. Fishing is another pastime for us. There is the Suwannee River and the Gulf of Mexico. We went to Cedar Key with Mike several times a month to fish on a pier by the Gulf of Mexico. Mike has been another friend of mine for over 60 years. A couple of times we took a charter boat out of Tarpon Springs and on occasion a charter boat out of Cedar Key.

There are auctions we like to attend also. We have been to nearly every restaurant in the seven-county area of Florida. Great food is in Florida.

There are several Wildlife Rescue farms. One has buffalo and rain deer, Several have horses, mules, and donkeys, and another one has camels, zebras, and peacocks.

The list goes on. Quite a few rescue organizations in Florida.

Reminiscing

So here I am. 78 years old looking back. I was married for over 51 years. It was a roller coaster for us. Perhaps the tragedy of losing our daughter caused the whirlwind in our lives. I must believe things would have been better had she not gotten ill. It's no one's fault. But the fact is that it happened, and life wasn't so easy. I will always have a special place in my heart for Ron. He was my childhood sweetheart and the father of my children.

I acquired more friends in Florida. Specifically, my friend Wanda. Wanda also lost her husband and was married a long time like me, so she was able to relate to the roller coaster of emotions that a widow goes through. While I was in Florida Wanda and I would go out to dinner and dance almost every day.

One of my friends, Mary from Ohio was also widowed out of a long-term marriage. I have known Mary for over

24 years and got to know her late husband Joe. Joe, Mary, me, and Ron all took trips to the Casino in Canada a few times. After Mary's husband Joe passed, Mary moved to Florida and lived there for quite a while before I was able to move to Florida. I had many friends to socialize with and to hang out with and do things together in Ohio and Florida. Rita was a friend who was always there for me.

I kept going to the gym to shed some of this weight so that I could feel better. I hoped to find someone that would travel to Florida with me.

The realization that he is gone was present but... I keep thinking that he will be returning.

Thanks to COVID-19 I met Rich. Rich was the only social being I was able to socialize with during the COVID-19 epidemic. I needed to socialize!!

Before I met Rich, I would always have to be doing something. I couldn't sleep. I couldn't stay in one place. I was obsessed with socializing. I kept wanting to meet someone to share my life with, but as soon as someone attempted to get intimate with me, I would back away. If it wasn't for COVID-19, I would have probably backed away from Rich. Rich did attempt to hook up with me a year earlier, but I declined his attention. I wasn't sure what I wanted back then. All my friends would say there was never a dull moment around me. That's because I was always searching without knowing what I was searching for. But now I realize, the reason I was going through this is because I was trying to find myself. I was trying to find a purpose for living.

Why did I feel the need to commute to Florida every winter? Why did I get up in the middle of the night always around 3:00 am? Why couldn't I sleep more than 2-4 hours at a time? What was the need to have someone around me at all times? I believe the answer to all the questions is that I was trying to fill that void in my life.

It would be unfair to compare Rich with my husband because we were two different couples in two different eras. I love Rich with all my heart and even though Ron and I had our ups and downs, I loved Ron. I believe that Ron has tried to reach out to me after he passed. The dreams I had and the seagull following my boat were just strange. There were too many spiritual incidents. If Ron truly was here in spirit and loved me, then he would be glad I am where I am today. Who knows, perhaps it was Ron's spirit that led us together. These two guys are alike in many ways and in many ways very different. They not only share the same woman, but they also even share the exact birthday.

Would I have loved Rich in my Teenage years like I did Ron? Would I have been as desirable to Rich as I was to Ron in my younger years? How would Ron have handled this COVID thing? How would Ron have handled my aging process? Would Rich have loved me as much then as he does now? Would he have desired me back in the day the way Ron desired me?

I will never know those answers, but one thing for sure I do know is that I am very content. I have not been this relaxed for many years. Rich has calmed me down in a magical way. I have always been the caregiver and now things are switched the other way. I feel like Rich is an angel looking over me.

Thanks to COVID-19 I am sharing the rest of my life with a very special caring person. I now have a purpose in life and more faith in God.

If COVID-19 was a germ warfare, then as far as I am concerned, this American won that war.